CW01302229

LEGENDS OF UKRAINE

Written by Liudmyla Pytel

Mountain Mill Editorial

Copyright © 2024 by Mountain Mill Editorial
All rights reserved.
No part of this publication may be reproduced, distributed, or transmitted in any form or by any means, including photocopying, recording, or other electronic or mechanical methods, without the prior written permission of the publisher, except as permitted by U.S. copyright law.
For permission requests, contact:
mountain.mill.editorial@gmail.com

Author Liudmyla Pytel

Third edition 2024

Prologue

Ukraine is a land where the whisper of the past mingles with the vibrant pulse of the present. Its rolling plains, majestic mountains, and ancient rivers cradle a history that is rich, complex, and deeply intertwined with its cultural folklore. These tales, passed down through generations, are not merely stories—they are reflections of the resilience, wisdom, and spirit of the Ukrainian people.

In these pages, you will journey through myths and legends that have stood the test of time. From the enigmatic forest spirits known as Mavkas to the valor of heroes like Bohdan Khmelnytsky, and from the awe-inspiring creation of the country's mountains to the poetic origins of the Big Dipper, each story reveals the heart of a nation that treasures its heritage and dares to dream.

This collection is more than an anthology; it is an invitation to step into the soul of Ukraine. Through these tales, you will uncover themes of bravery, love, justice, and hope—values that continue to inspire and unite people across the ages.

As you delve into these legends, may you feel the magic and the wonder of a land where history breathes and myths come alive. May you carry with you not only the stories but also the enduring spirit of Ukraine.

Welcome to the legends. Welcome to Ukraine.

We dedicate this book to the Ukrainian people. They love their land with all their heart and defend it like true heroes.

The best times are yet to come!

Contents

THE MAVKAS: GUARDIANS OF THE FORESTS 7

THE CHALLENGE OF THE IRON HORSE 13

THE LEGEND OF PRINCE IGOR 19

ILYA MUROMETS AND THE THREE-HEADED DRAGON 23

THE TREASURE OF PRINCESS OLGA 27

THE HIDDEN CITY 32

THE SWORD OF BOHDAN KHMELNYTSKY 37

THE LEGEND OF HOVERLA MOUNTAIN 42

THE LION OF LVIV 47

THE UKRAINIAN TREASURE 51

THREE GUARDIANS OF UKRAINE 53

THE CREATION OF THE WORLD 57

VYRIY AND THE TREE OF LIFE 61

THE BIRTH OF THE CARPATHIAN MOUNTAINS 64

THE BEAR MOUNTAIN 75

DIVA'S ROCK, MONK'S ROCK, AND CAT'S MOUNTAIN 83

THE LEGEND OF THE BIG DIPPER 91

THE MYSTERY OF THE MOON 94

WHY IS SEAWATER SALTY? 97

HOW A MOTHER BECAME A CUCKOO 101

WHERE IS THE TRUE HAPPINESS? 106

THE LEGEND OF DESTINY 115

LEAF AND GOLD 120

FOUNDERS OF KYIV 126

The Mavkas: Guardians of the Forests

In the heart of magical Ukraine, there are stories and legends as ancient as the forests and rivers that adorn its beautiful landscape. One such legend is that of the Mavkas, the mysterious creatures who reside in the lush forests of the Carpathian Mountains.

The Mavkas are female spirits that appear as beautiful young women with long, shiny hair, and large, expressive eyes. They cast no shadow nor reflection, and despite their human appearance, their backs are hollow, a sign that they are not of our world. They are said to be the souls of girls who departed from this world too early and now live in the forests, caring for and protecting them.

One day, a boy named Yuri ventured into the forest to gather wood for the winter. It was a sunny day, perfect for exploring and playing. As he delved deeper and deeper into the forest, he lost his way among the tall trees and winding paths. It was getting dark, and Yuri began to feel afraid.

Suddenly, he heard a melodious song. He followed the voice to a clearing, where he saw a group of beautiful young women dancing in a circle. They were the Mavkas, although Yuri didn't know it at that moment. Drawn in by their beauty and their music, Yuri approached.

The Mavkas stopped when they saw him. They looked at the lost boy with curiosity and kindness. One of them, the tallest one with hair golden like the sun, stepped forward.

"You are lost, little human," she said.

Yuri nodded, his eyes filled with wonder and a little fear.

"Do not be afraid," said the Mavka, her voice soft as a song. "We can help you get back home. But first, you must promise us something."

Yuri frowned. "What must I promise?"

"You must promise us that you will take care of this forest. That you will not harm it and that you will protect its inhabitants, be they animals or plants. If you make this promise, we will show you the way home," said the Mavka.

Yuri nodded quickly. "I promise," he said, and the Mavkas smiled.

True to their word, the Mavkas helped Yuri get out of the forest. When Yuri looked back from the edge of the forest, the Mavkas had disappeared, leaving only the melody of their song floating in the air.

Yuri never forgot his encounter with the Mavkas nor the promise he made. He grew up to become a caretaker of the forest, protecting and respecting nature, and teaching others to do the same. He always remembered the song of the Mavkas, a reminder of the mysterious guardians of the forest and the promise he had made.

The legend of the Mavkas teaches us the importance of respecting and protecting nature, and it reminds us that our world is full of mysteries and wonders waiting to be discovered. So, the next time you're in a forest, pay attention. Who knows? Perhaps you'll hear the melody of the Mavkas, reminding you of the promise to care for and respect our wonderful world.

The Challenge of the Iron Horse

In the plains of Ukraine, where wheat fields dance with the wind and rivers snake through lush meadows, an ancient legend is told that of the Iron Horse. A tale of bravery, cunning, and endurance that has withstood the test of time.

Many centuries ago, in a small village, a monster appeared. It was a horse made entirely of iron, with eyes of fire and hooves that rumbled like thunder. It terrorized the village, destroying crops and houses with its metal fury.

The villagers tried to fight the beast, but their swords and arrows couldn't pierce its iron skin.

Despair took hold of the village, and the inhabitants resigned themselves to living in constant fear of the Iron Horse.

Except for one. Ivan, a young shepherd, decided that enough was enough. Though he was small and did not have the strength of a warrior, he possessed great bravery and unparalleled cunning.

Ivan ventured to the blacksmith's workshop and worked for days and nights, forging a long iron chain. The blacksmith, impressed by his determination, helped him finish the chain and gave him his blessing.

With the chain in hand, Ivan headed to the field where the Iron Horse usually roamed. When the monster appeared, Ivan ran towards it, dodging its kicks and snorts. With a cry of defiance, he threw the chain around the beast's neck. The Iron Horse snorted and shook, but the chain held firm.

But Ivan knew he couldn't hold the monster forever. He needed a way to extinguish the horse's fire eyes and calm its fury. He remembered an old well in the village that had been dry for years. If he could lead the Iron Horse there, perhaps he could use the underground water to extinguish its fiery eyes.

With all his strength, Ivan pulled the chain and guided the Iron Horse towards the well. It was an exhausting struggle, with the monster resisting every step. But Ivan didn't give in.

Finally, they arrived at the well. Ivan, with one last effort, pushed the Iron Horse into the well. The weight of the horse on the bottom of the well caused the underground water to gush out, extinguishing the beast's fiery eyes and cooling its iron body.

From that day on, the Iron Horse no longer terrorized the village. Ivan had proven that even the most fearsome of monsters can be defeated with bravery and cunning. And although he was just a young shepherd, he became a hero in his village, reminding everyone that there is no challenge they cannot face.

The Legend of Prince Igor

In the rich lands of ancient Ukraine, the story of a brave leader named Prince Igor was told. As the ruler of the powerful land of Ukraine, Igor's bravery and wisdom were known throughout the country.

Igor's most famous story began when he

decided to embark on a campaign against the nomadic Cumans, who had been threatening his lands. Accompanied by his loyal army, Prince Igor marched east, determined to protect his people.

However, things did not go as Igor had hoped. In the battle that ensued, Igor's forces were overwhelmed by the Cumans, and he was captured and taken prisoner.

Despite his dire situation, Igor remained strong. During his captivity, he displayed great resilience and dignity, refusing to bow to his captors. His courage impressed the Cumans so much that they treated him with respect, though they did not set him free.

But Igor was not destined to remain a prisoner forever. After several years in captivity, he managed to escape. He crossed deserts and mountains, evading the Cuman hunters and enduring the harsh climate, until he finally managed to reach his home.

Igor's return was met with joy and celebration. His people welcomed him as a hero, with his wife Yaroslavna and son Volodymyr leading the way. From that day on, he became a symbol of resistance and bravery, a reminder that even in the darkest moments, one must maintain hope and fight for freedom.

The story of Prince Igor has been told and retold over the years, becoming a beloved legend in Ukraine. His brave spirit and his love for his land continue to inspire people to this day, reminding them of the power of resilience and the importance of fighting for what one believes in.

Ilya Muromets and the Three-Headed Dragon

A long time ago, in ancient Ukraine, in a humble home in a small village, lived a boy named Ilya. Although he was born strong and healthy, a mysterious illness left him unable to walk at the age of three. He spent the next thirty years in bed, dreaming of adventures and feats of bravery.

One day, two mysterious travelers arrived at Ilya's home. They turned out to be disguised gods, who offered him a magical liquid. Upon drinking it, Ilya miraculously healed and gained superhuman strength. He stood up and transformed into a robust giant, ready to embark on heroic adventures.

Armed with his new strength, Ilya left his home and headed to the great city of Kyiv. On his way, he defeated several monsters and bandits terrorizing the country's people, gaining fame and respect.

Eventually, he arrived in Kyiv and presented himself to Prince Vladimir, the city's ruler. The prince was impressed by Ilya's feats and invited him to join his noble warriors, the Bogatyrs.

As one of the Bogatyrs, Ilya faced many

challenges and battles. But none was more dangerous than his confrontation with the fearsome Zmey Gorynych, a three-headed dragon terrorizing the land.

Ilya bravely fought against the dragon, using his incredible strength to overcome the monster's flames and claws. After a long and exhausting battle, Ilya managed to defeat Zmey Gorynych, freeing the land from its tyranny.

The brave Ilya Muromets became a beloved hero throughout the land, and his adventures were told from generation to generation. Although he eventually died in battle, his spirit was never forgotten. To this day, his story inspires people to be brave and to fight against injustices, demonstrating that even the most discouraging circumstances can be overcome with courage and determination.

The Treasure of Princess Olga

Ukraine is a land of tales and legends, and among them all, the Treasure of Princess Olga holds a special place. This is a story of bravery, wisdom, and a hidden treasure, a story that continues to be told on warm Ukrainian nights.

Many centuries ago, Olga was the ruler of the

city of Kyiv. She was known not only for her beauty but also for her wisdom and courage. Under her leadership, Kyiv flourished and became a rich and powerful city.

But one day, the city was threatened by an invading army. Olga knew she couldn't fight them, and that the city was in grave danger. However, instead of surrendering, she devised a plan.

Princess Olga had a treasure, a vast collection of jewels, gold, and valuable artifacts that the city had accumulated over the years. She decided to hide the treasure so that it wouldn't fall into enemy hands.

For three nights, Olga and her most loyal followers worked in secret, digging a deep hole in an unknown location within the city. On the fourth day, as the sun was just beginning to peek over the horizon, Princess Olga's treasure was finally buried.

Then, Olga confronted the invading army, but instead of fighting, she offered to surrender and hand over the city in exchange for the safety of her people. The enemy, expecting the treasure of Kyiv, agreed. But when they searched for the treasure, they found only a city empty of riches.

Enraged, the invaders threatened Olga, but she stood firm. "The true treasure of Kyiv is not in jewels or gold, but in its people. And that is a treasure you can never take," she declared.

Eventually, the invaders left, leaving the city intact. And although Kyiv had lost its material treasure, its people were safe. And Olga, she would be remembered as the wise princess who saved her people.

Since then, the location of Princess Olga's Treasure has remained a mystery. Many have searched, but no one has found the resting place of Kyiv's riches. The legend says that only when Kyiv is at its darkest hour will the treasure be discovered once again to save the city.

The legend of Princess Olga's Treasure is a story of sacrifice and wisdom. It teaches us that the true treasure of a city is not found in its riches but in the bravery and wisdom of its people. And that no matter what happens, there will always be hope in the darkest times.

The Hidden City

In the vast and mysterious land of Ukraine, an ancient legend was told about a hidden city, concealed deep within the Carpathian Mountains.

According to the legend, many centuries ago, there was a beautiful city named Zolota, built with walls of gold and roofs of silver, shining with a light so bright that it could be seen from miles away. The city was home to wise and fair people, but over time, the envy of enemies for its wealth and beauty put it in danger.

To protect themselves, the citizens of Zolota turned to their most powerful magician, an old man named Mykola. Mykola conjured a powerful spell that made the city disappear, hiding it inside a mountain. But the spell came at a price: it could only be undone by someone of pure heart who did not desire Zolota's wealth for themselves.

For centuries, the location of Zolota remained a mystery. Many sought the hidden city, drawn by tales of its wealth, but none could find it.

One day, a young shepherd named Ivan encountered an old woman in the forest. The old woman was tired and hungry, and Ivan, despite his poverty, shared his food with her. Grateful, the old woman revealed her true identity: she was the guardian of Zolota, sent to find someone worthy of entering the city.

The old woman led Ivan to the mountain where Zolota was hidden. There, Ivan proved his bravery and purity of heart by rejecting the offer of Zolota's wealth for himself. Instead, he asked that the city and its people be freed from their confinement.

Moved by his generosity, the old woman undid the spell, and Zolota reappeared in all its splendor. The people of the city freed after so many centuries, celebrated their freedom and chose Ivan as their new leader, grateful for his courage and kindness.

The story of Zolota and Ivan became a legend, passed down from generation to generation. And even though Zolota eventually faded into history, its story lives on in the heart of the Ukrainian people, reminding them of the value of kindness, humility, and courage in the face of greed and adversity.

The Sword of Bohdan Khmelnytsky

One of the most prominent figures in Ukrainian history is Bohdan Khmelnytsky, a Cossack leader known for his courage and strategic skill. Although there are many factual accounts of his exploits, he has also become a character in legends and folktales. One of the most famous stories is that of his magical sword.

It was said that Bohdan Khmelnytsky possessed a special sword, a gift from the ancient Slavic gods. It wasn't particularly large or lavish, but it had a unique quality: it never failed in battle. Each time Khmelnytsky wielded it, the sword found its target and its owner emerged victorious.

This sword was a constant pillar in Khmelnytsky's battles against Ukraine's enemies, and its fame spread so much that enemy soldiers trembled in fear at seeing it unsheathed.

However, the sword wasn't just an instrument of war. According to legend, it also had the power to point out the correct direction when Khmelnytsky was at a crossroads or needed to make a difficult decision. He would simply place the sword on the ground, and the blade would spin and point in the direction he should take.

One day, during an especially fierce battle, Khmelnytsky was separated from his army and found himself surrounded by enemies. With no way out in sight, he drew his sword and placed it on the ground. To his surprise, the sword didn't point in any escape direction but pointed directly at the approaching enemies.

Khmelnytsky understood the message: he should not run but face his enemies. With a cry of defiance, he threw himself into the battle, his sword cutting the air with lethal precision.

Despite being outnumbered, he fought with such ferocity that the enemies were forced to retreat. In the end, he was rescued by his men, who had been drawn by the heat of the battle.

Since that day, the story of Khmelnytsky's magical sword has been told throughout Ukraine. Although a lot of time has passed since then, and the sword has been lost to history, the legend endures.

The story of Bohdan Khmelnytsky's sword is a lesson in bravery and wisdom. It teaches us that, even when we are surrounded by challenges and the odds are against us, we must face them with courage. And while a magical sword can be helpful, it's the indomitable spirit of a true leader that really matters in battle.

The Legend of Hoverla Mountain

In the beautiful land of Ukraine stands Hoverla Mountain, the highest in the entire country. Throughout the centuries, a fascinating legend has been woven about this majestic mountain.

The story goes that many centuries ago, in a valley near the mountain, lived a charming maiden named Olena. Her beauty was such that men from all regions came to ask for her hand in marriage. But Olena only had eyes for a young hunter named Danylo, famous for his bravery and kindness.

Danylo and Olena were deeply in love and wished to marry. However, a powerful and cruel feudal lord was also smitten by Olena's beauty and filled with jealousy, challenged Danylo to a test of bravery. The test was to climb Hoverla Mountain, something that no one had ever accomplished before. Danylo, guided by his love for Olena, accepted the challenge. In his ascent, he battled against snowstorms, sliding rocks, and freezing winds. His courage and determination were strong, but the mountain was a formidable opponent.

After many days and nights, he finally reached the summit. From there, he looked out at the world around him, with the sight of beautiful Ukraine stretching out in all directions. But his triumph was short-lived, as a freezing wind blew and, exhausted and unprotected, Danylo succumbed to the cold.

When Danylo did not return, Olena was distraught. With a heart filled with sorrow and determination, she decided to climb the mountain to find her beloved. She fought against the same challenges, but her love and her pain strengthened her, and she finally made it to the top.

There, she found Danylo, frozen but with a smile of peace on his face. Filled with sadness, Olena wept and her tears, mixing with the snow, turned into a small stream flowing down the mountain.

Since then, it is said that this stream, known as Olena's Tear, still flows on Hoverla. The mountain became a symbol of bravery and true love. And though Danylo and Olena could not be together in life, their love endures in the legend, reminding all who hear their story that true love never dies, and that courage and determination should always be remembered and celebrated.

The Lion of Lviv

The charming city of Lviv, known as the "city of lions," has a rich history and many legends intertwined with its past. One of the most famous is the legend of the Lion of Lviv.

The story goes that many centuries ago when Lviv was just a small settlement, it was constantly threatened by bands of invaders seeking to plunder it. One day, a large invading army approached the city, ready to destroy everything in its path.

When news of the imminent attack reached the city's king, he was desperate. He knew his men were not enough to defend the city. In his desperation, he prayed to the ancient Slavic gods, asking for protection for his people.

The gods, moved by the king's plea, decided to help. They transformed one of the city's lion statues into a real lion. With a roar that shook the mountains and a golden glow in its eyes, the lion leaped from its pedestal and ran toward the invading army.

The invaders, upon seeing the gigantic lion, fell into panic. They tried to fight, but the lion's claws and teeth were stronger than any sword or spear. In no time, the invaders were defeated and forced to flee, leaving Lviv in peace.

When the battle ended, the lion returned to the city. Before the astonished eyes of the inhabitants, it returned to its statue form, resplendent in the afternoon sun.

Since that day, the people of Lviv have held a deep respect and love for lions. Lion statues can be found throughout the city, reminding everyone of the bravery of the Lion of Lviv that once protected their home.

The legend of the Lion of Lviv is a tale of protection and bravery. Although it is just a story, it captures the spirit of the city of Lviv: a place that values its history takes pride in its resilience and is always ready to face the challenges that come its way.

The Ukrainian Treasure

This happened in times when God distributed the treasures of the world among the nations, bestowing upon each country the riches of the earth. God's bounty was vast and varied, with treasures ranging from glittering diamonds and great gold mines to fertile plains and deep forests teeming with life and abundance.

Once the distribution was complete, God noticed a young woman in simple clothes, secluded and sad, with no gifts in her hands. He saw that the girl represented an entire country and contemplated what he should bestow upon the young woman.

"To you, pure-hearted one, I will give the most precious thing I possess: music."

And so, the young woman, filled with enthusiasm and joy, spread this magical gift through the centuries.

This young woman is the image of our glorious Ukraine, which everyone now recognizes as a country with an incomparable wealth of songs that spring from the heart and soul of its people.

Three Guardians of Ukraine

In a time long ago, the Earth was a vast and boundless place where beauty and harmony reigned supreme. The land brimmed with breathtaking landscapes, and the air was perfumed with the scent of wildflowers. The rivers flowed gently through the meadows, their blue waters glistening in the sunlight. Animals roamed free, and the people lived in peace and tranquility. It was a world unlike any other, where every corner of the Earth was a canvas of unparalleled beauty.

But some people did not appreciate the serenity, so they decided to attack and conquer these lands. The land, once full of flowers, turned red with the blood of innocent people.

The remaining people cried out to the Earth for help, beseeching their mother to protect them. In desperation, they called to Mother Earth: "Protect us, our mother!"

When the enemies began to extract treasures and wished to head north, a great, ancient forest blocked their path. Attempting to go west, they encountered massive mountains that were insurmountable. And moving south, they fell into a vast chasm that was filled by the sea's

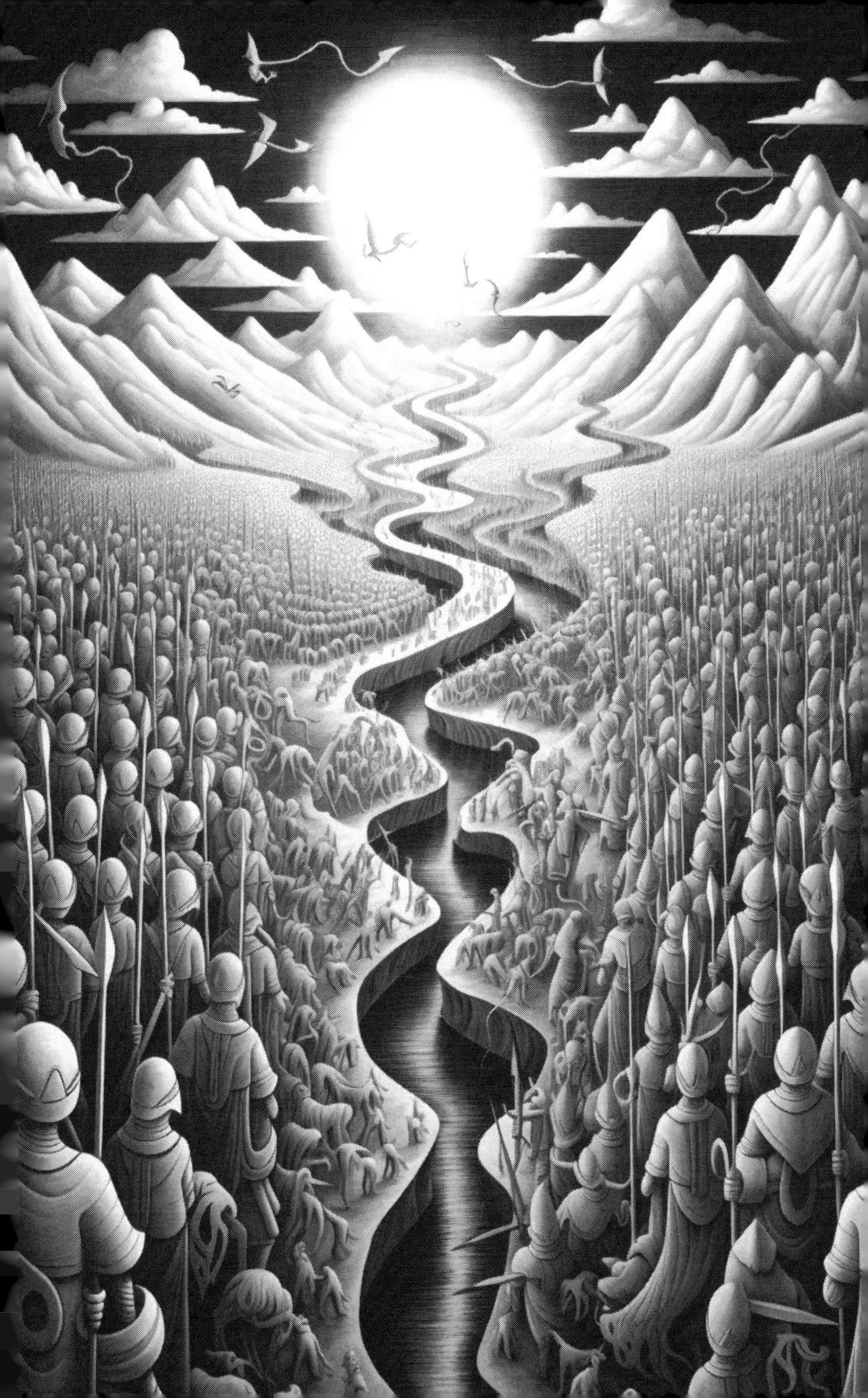

waters.

Thus, the Earth sheltered her children with three guardians: an impenetrable forest in the north, towering mountains in the west, and the expansive Black Sea to the south.

Those who come bearing malice will find themselves lost in its vastness, but those who are righteous will always be welcomed with bread and salt.

The Creation of the World

Since the beginning of time, everything was shrouded in darkness. In this boundless wasteland, where neither time nor space existed, The Eye was the sole dwelling entity.

Then, one day, a solitary tear from The Eye transformed into a golden-winged hawk. As it

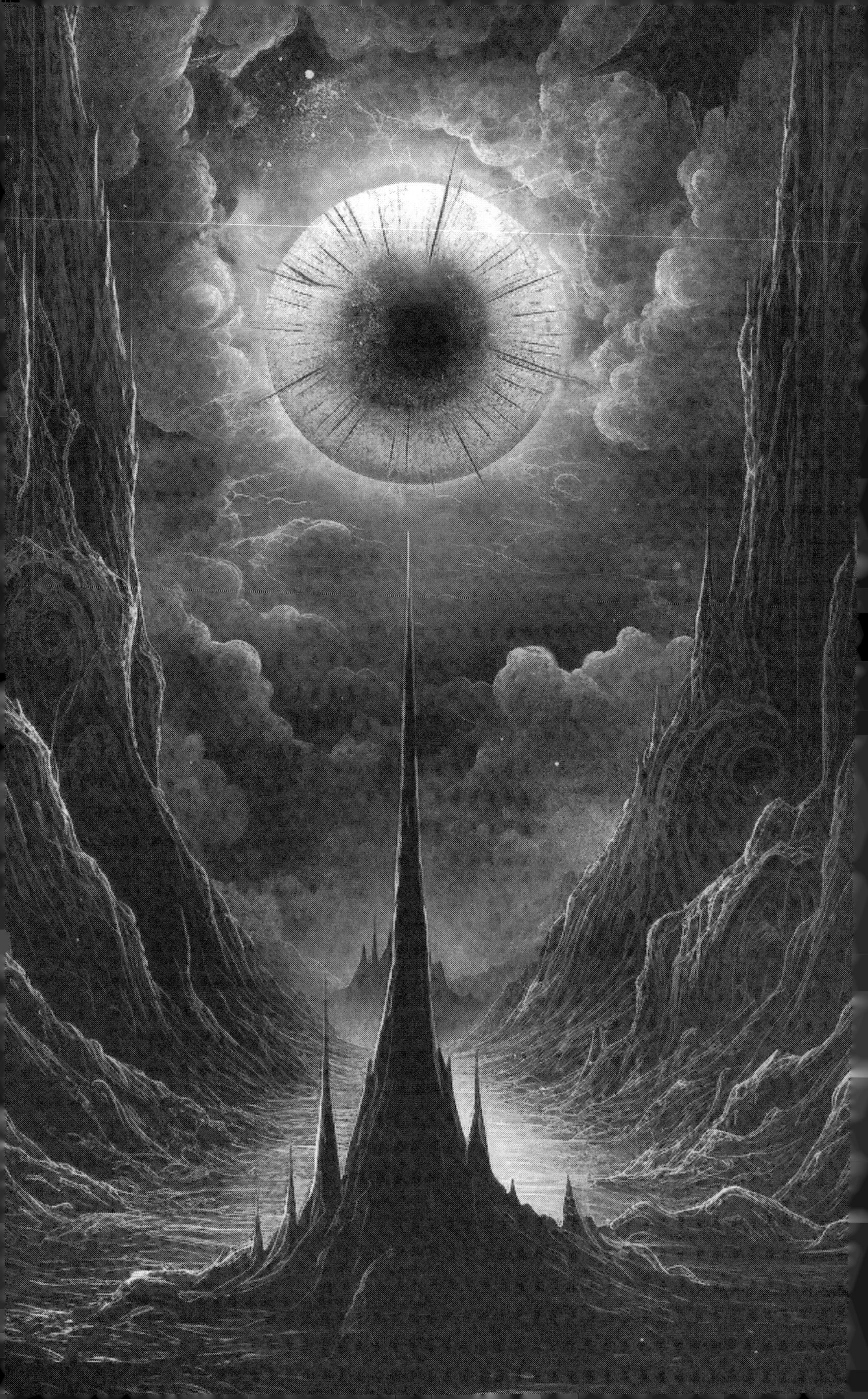

spread its wings and flew through the darkness, the earth emerged beneath. Nourished by the waters of a spring originating from its beak, a tree grew tall and strong. Upon one of its branches, The Hawk laid two eggs, one white and one black.

From the white egg, a swan emerged that drank from the spring, becoming the God Belobog, the spirit of light. From the black egg, another swan was born, becoming the God Chernobog, the lord of darkness.

The Hawk addressed them, saying, "I have given you life and the gift of creation. Fill this world with beauty and harmony." In response, Belobog created light, warmth, and goodness, as well as the sun, rivers, and groves. Chernobog brought forth the moon and stars, darkness, and the seeds of evil.

The Hawk decreed that day follows night, the

Moon rises in the sun's absence, and good contends with evil. And so, it was to be for eternity. Together, they brought forth life, and thus humans were born, embodying the bright and dark traits of both gods, good and evil.

The Hawk blessed humanity with reason, enabling them to distinguish light from darkness, good from evil. In their gratitude, they named him Rod, the progenitor of all living things.

Since the beginning of time, everything has been shrouded in darkness. In this boundless wasteland, where neither time nor space existed, The Eye was the only dwelling being.

Vyriy and the Tree of Life

The Earth is our mother and protector, possessing incomparable strength. Every year, during the summer months, she tirelessly bestows upon us her bounties: sweet berries, delicious fruits, and nutritious grains.

But, like any mother, she also needs rest. As autumn arrives, her strength wanes. Nature withers and falls into a deep slumber.

Feeling the changes, birds gather in large flocks and embark on a long journey toward the mysterious place where the Tree of Life grows, a sanctuary of eternal warmth. This sacred tree stands in the midst of perpetual spring, its branches reaching towards the heavens, grazing the stars.

Vyriy is a paradisiacal realm where time flows uniquely. The waters from its springs are pristine and healing, and even the Sun and Moon repose in its treetop.

Upon arrival, the birds rest and exchange tales with the human souls dwelling there in harmony and peace. It is said that on Christmas Eve, the birds lend their wings to these souls, allowing them to visit their earthly families, to bask in the warmth of home, and to hear familiar melodies.

With the onset of the new year, as nature stirs from its winter repose, the cuckoo, wielding celestial keys, seals away the cold season. Larks soar to herald the arrival of spring, followed by other birds in procession.

Swallows carry happiness on their wings, nightingales bring forth new songs, and storks bear the souls of children, ready to be born, to weave new threads of life.

The Birth of the Carpathian Mountains

Once upon a time, there was an endless vast plain in our land of Ukraine. The plain was green with silky grasses, evergreen firs, mighty beeches, sycamores, birches, and poplars. Streams and rivers flowed, rich with all kinds of life.

The lord of the valley was a giant named Silun whose steps made the ground shake as he walked. It was said that Silun was skilled in farming and had much livestock of every kind. Herds of cows, oxen, sheep, horses, buffaloes, and pigs grazed in the fields and roamed the forests.

Silun resided in a splendid palace of white marble, the towers of which rose to the point of touching the clouds.

This palace, with countless rooms, was a labyrinth in which it was easy to get lost. Within its walls were countless treasures and wonders.

At night, Silun slept on a golden bed lined with expensive carpets. And during the day he often rested in a silver chair. In the majestic valleys, Silun's servants cared for the land, harvesting wheat, and tending to the livestock.

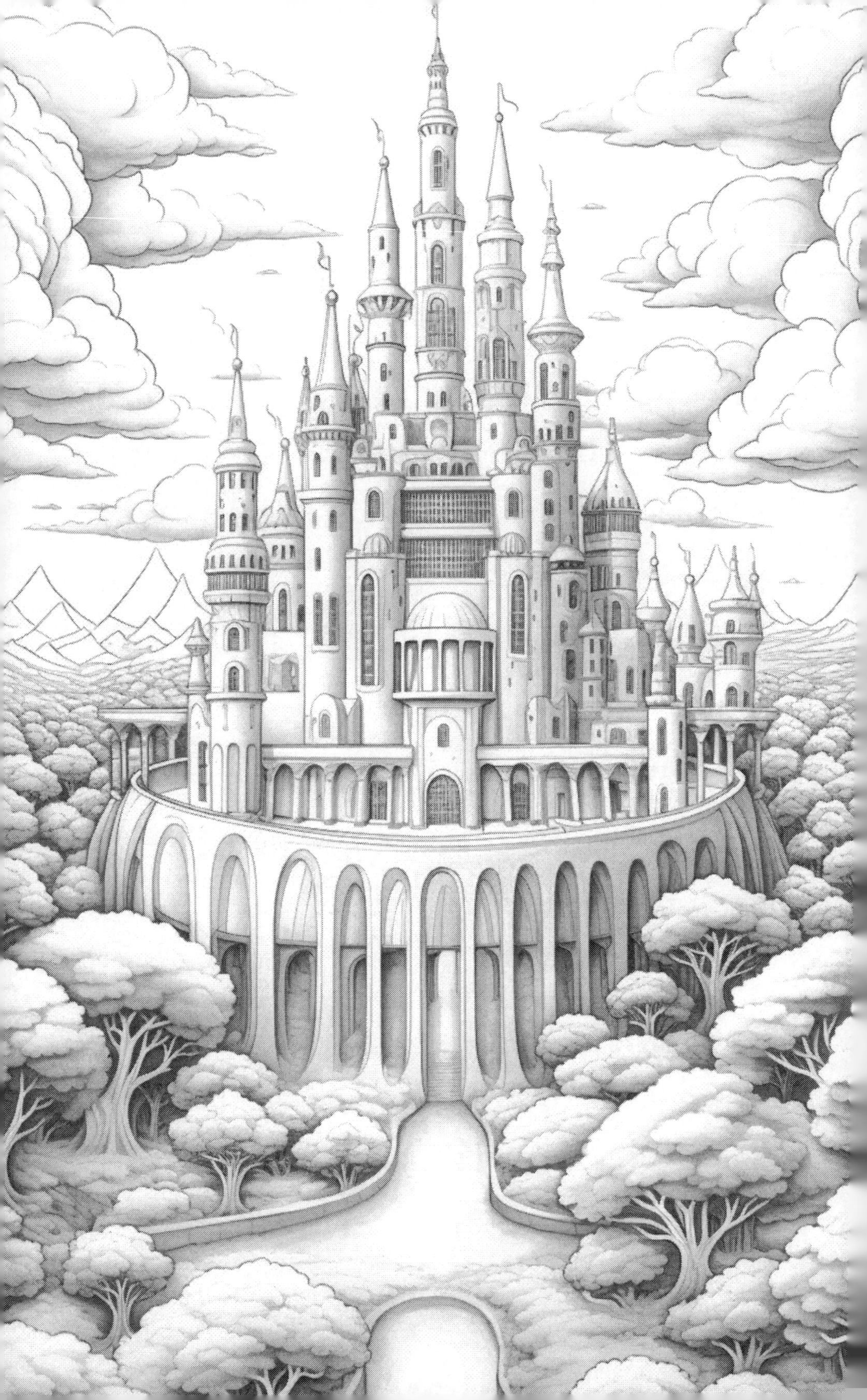

The people were tormented, they worked from dawn to dusk, multiplying riches, but not for themselves, for Silun.

The servants lived far from the palace, in simple wooden huts because Silun did not want the rooms to stink of human sweat. Nobody dared to leave Silun's lands in search of other work. They had to live and die as servants.

Among these servants was a young man named Carpo Dneprovsky, who had come here from the banks of the Dnieper. At ten, he went on a journey seeking fortune to help his mother. She lived in poverty because her husband, Carpo's father, had died.

Carpo worked as Silun's servant for many years. Like everyone else, he mowed the grass, plowed, and sowed wheat, rye, barley, and oats, besides baking bread.

In addition to working on his tasks assigned by Silun, he also helped others, because he felt sorry for the weak. All the servants loved him for his honesty, fairness, and hard work.

Carpo hated those who bowed at the Lord's feet. It was hard for him to see how Silun took everything, and the people starved.

When Carpo turned twenty, he decided to return home. He didn't plan to go back to his mother empty-handed and was sure that his master would pay him for the good work done over so many years.

One night he went out to cool off and saw a shadow he immediately recognized. It was Silun. It was the perfect moment to speak to his lord.

"Why are you here, Carpo?" asked Silun, recognizing the boy. "Are you waiting for some girl?"

"Not a girl," replied Carpo, "but you, my lord. I have served you for a long time, but I must go home to find my mother alive and would like to ask for payment for my service."

At first, Silun thought the servant was joking since no one had dared to ask for anything before. Carpo continued.

"I served honestly, sir. And my work, I believe, is worth something."

"You're not going anywhere! I own you, and I

command your life."

"I will go, sir," insisted Carpo, "but once more I must tell you that my work is worth something."

It was an unheard-of audacity, Silun had never heard such insolence. He could not allow it.

"I'm going to kill you and bury you right here! Your salary is there," he said, pointing down and approaching the young man.

But the boy did not step back.

"You will have to pay for my work, sir," he reminded him again. This response enraged Silun even more, whose anger boiled to the point that his eyes filled with blood and flames emerged from his mouth.

He grabbed Carpo with his strong hands, lifted him into the air, and threw him to the ground with such force that a deep crack formed in the ground.

But inexplicably, the servant was unharmed, stood up, and felt an invincible strength within himself. Apparently, Mother Earth was helping him, endowing him with unparalleled strength.

Carpo grabbed Silun, struck him on the ground, over and over again until Mother Earth couldn't take those hits, and the crack opened much more, creating a large cave, where Silun fell.

Silun tried to surface, but the ground was closing in on him. And so, Silun found himself buried, precisely what he had intended to do with his servant.

Because of the giant's strikes, mountains and valleys slowly formed. The harder Silun hit the Earth in his effort to free himself from captivity, the higher the mountains rose around him.

The area that received the strongest blows

was where the Hutsul region is located, and there the highest mountains were formed.

In the morning, when the servants woke up and saw what had happened, they were very surprised. There were mountains everywhere, and where the giant's palace once stood, there was now a gigantic abyss, undoubtedly created by the giant's desperate attempts to escape from the cave.

Water sprang from the earth and filled that abyss.

The people, now free, decided to start a new life. Some settled on the plains, others went to the mountains. They plowed, sowed, grew grain, and cared for livestock. They learned to fell forests and to build houses.

The lake was named Synevyr for its intense blue color, similar to that of the sky.

And in honor of Carpo, the surrounding mountains were called the Carpathians.

They say that Silun is still restless underground, and occasionally the thuds of the giant can be heard. But Silun, now aged, no longer moves mountains; his former power has disappeared forever. He will never come to the surface again!

The Bear Mountain

In ancient times, along the Crimean coast, resilient people lived a life of hard labor and exhausting work. Cruel and relentless gods reigned over them from the sky, demanding obedience and sacrifices of bulls, sheep, and other animals.

The people cleared dense forests, removed stones from mountain slopes, uncovered springs, and planted gardens and vineyards. The relentless advance of human determination pushed back the forests and subdued the mountains.

Gradually, life improved, and the people began to trust in their own strength, no longer submitting to the whims of their gods.

When the gods perceived that the coastal dwellers no longer seemed to require their oversight, they were incensed. For three days and nights, ominous black clouds gathered, thunder growled with menace, and a tempest brewed at sea.

Yet, the people were unshaken. Fishermen had braved storms, shepherds had endured mountain tempests, and farmers had seen their soil washed away by torrents, but they had

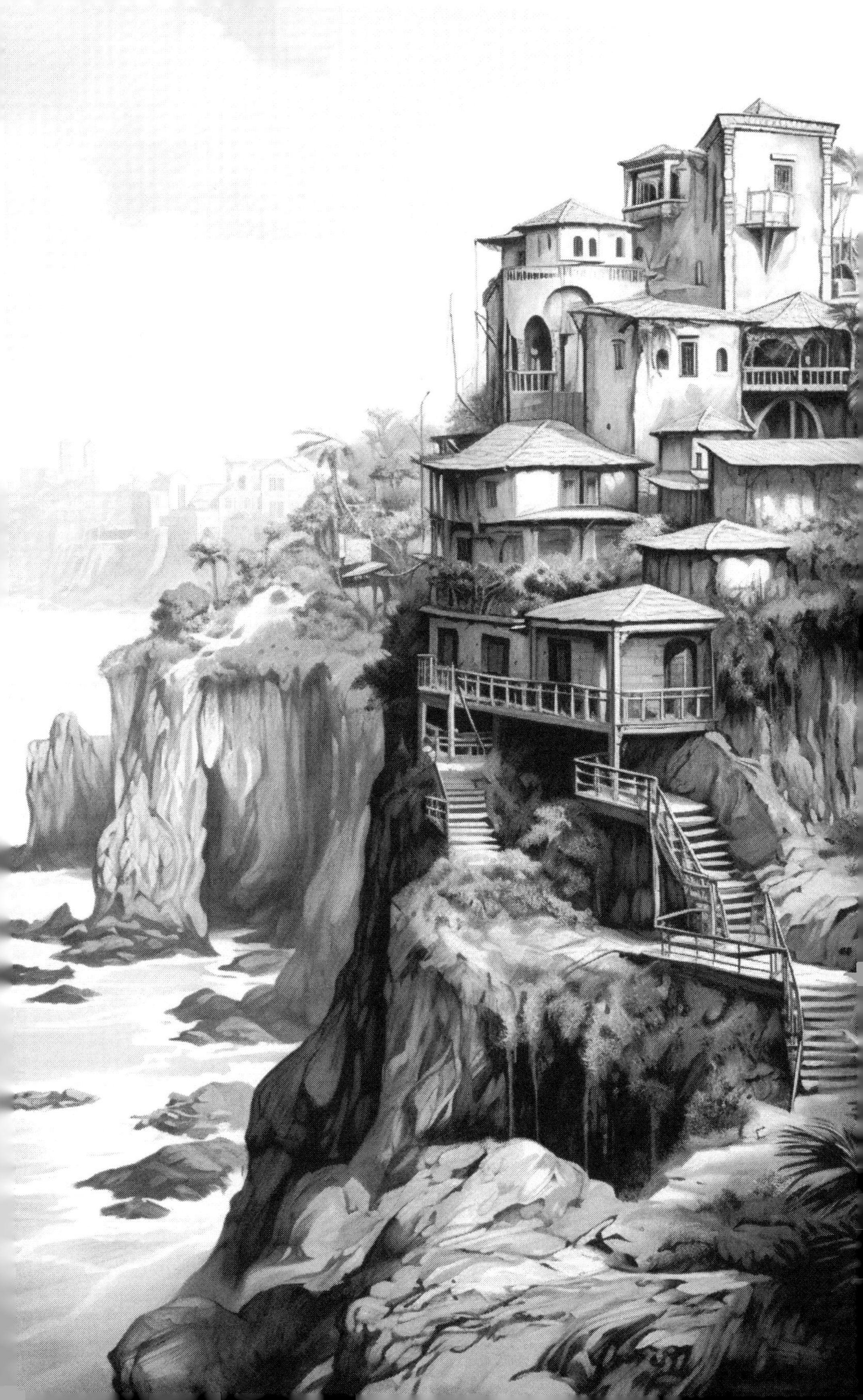

always persevered. Once more, humanity prevailed; the storm subsided, the sun returned, and the sea grew calm.

The gods, irate at their dwindling influence over humanity, bellowed, "Without us, life on this earth cannot persist! We will obliterate all until nothing but dust remains!"

Their gaze turned north, to the constellation known as *Ursa Major* (the Great Bear). By their will, they brought this cluster of stars to life, creating a colossal and threatening bear.

This celestial beast was directed southward to punish humankind. As the bear made its way across the sea, the gods looked on, anticipating destruction.

The bear-shaped creature approached the Crimean coast, emerged from the depths of the water, and stood on land on its legs. It was as big, heavy, and terrifying as a mountain. Its thick fur was like a dense forest, its ribs stood out like rocks, and water ran down its body like streams and waterfalls in the forest. The creature was so gigantic that its back reached the clouds. Emerging from the water, the creature caused waves so large that several

villages were completely swept away.

The bear marched on, destroying everything in its path with its immense weight. Its terrible paws crushed everything they encountered, and its sharp claws dug into the earth, leaving behind deep ravines and gorges.

Under the weight of the bear's body, the slopes of the Crimean Mountains collapsed, and the solid rocky subsoil gave way. It destroyed rocks and entire mountains, scattering debris around.

In the place where the city of Yalta's valley now lies, the bear exerted all its strength, pounding with its heavy paws and furiously scratching with its claws. Mountains, deep valleys, and wide depressions were created where there had been hills and gentle slopes before.

However, upon reaching the verdant valley of

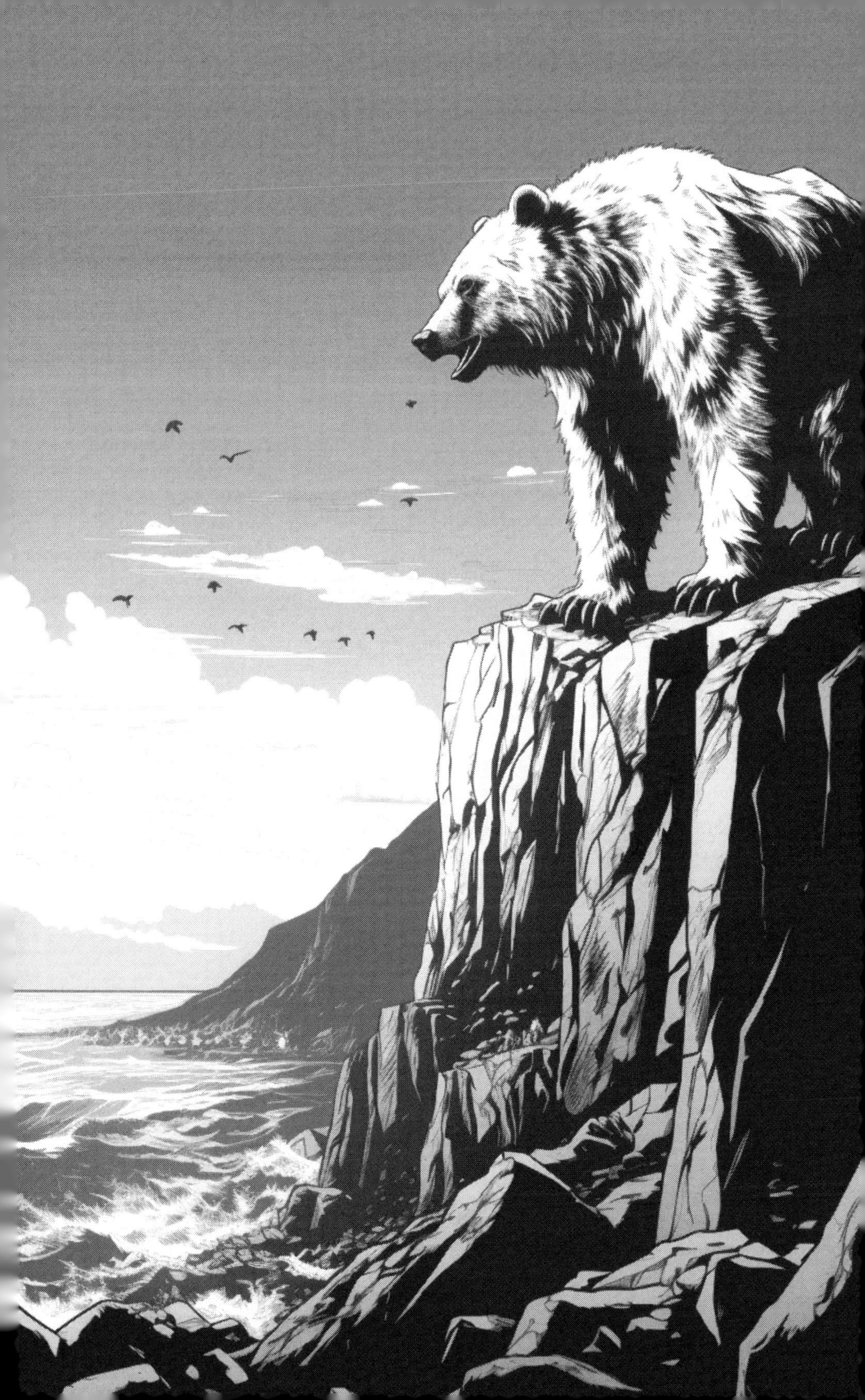

Partenit, with its lush gardens and vineyards, the creature's heart softened. It decided to live there, eternally delighting in the charming landscape, breathing the sea air, and bathing in the warm waters of the Black Sea.

The gods saw that the titan, once under their command, no longer obeyed them and understood that humanity had emerged victorious.

In a final act, they petrified the bear into a massive mountain, and thus Bear Mountain came to be, standing as a testament to the unyielding spirit of the Ukrainians.

Diva's Rock, Monk's Rock, and Cat's Mountain

In ancient times, the southern coast was shrouded by thick forests, with human settlements linked by narrow paths. Amidst the desolate rocks of Simeiz, a monk appeared.

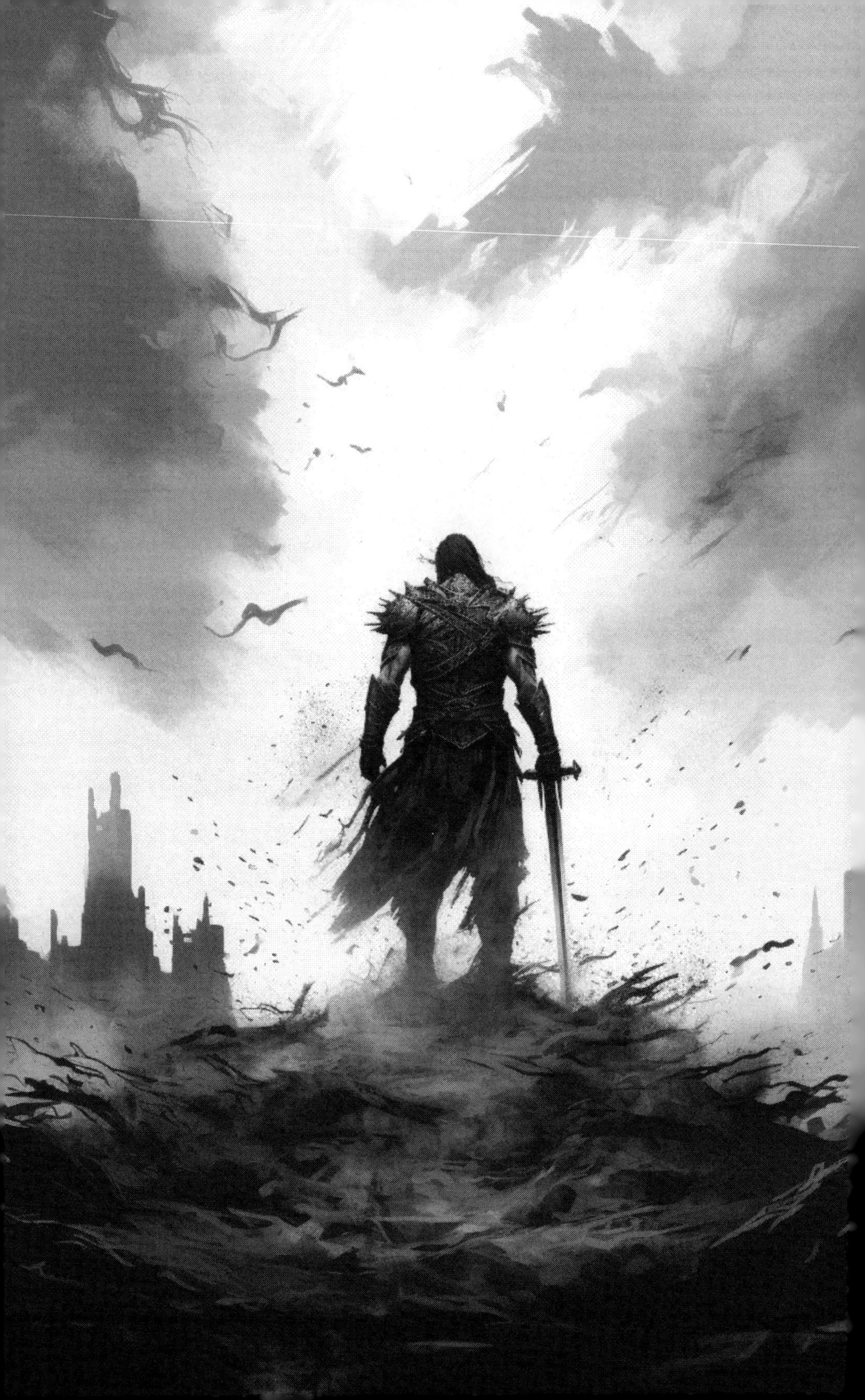

For a long while, his identity remained unknown, but whispers of his past life, filled with terrible deeds, circulated among the people.

Rumors told of a merciless warrior who, for years, had ravaged countries with fire and sword, destroyed cities, burned villages, and left behind a trail of death and despair.

Tormented by the apparitions of his victims, who cried out for revenge, he sought penance for their crimes. He found solace in a cave among the rocks of Simeiz, subsisting on wild fruits and occasional fish, fasting in hopes of forgetting his sins.

As years slipped by, memories of the hermit's past faded. The newer generations revered him as a wise and blameless man. Shepherds, catching glimpses of him, believed they saw a halo, a testament to his supposed sanctity.

Years of solitude made him forget much of his past. He began to believe he had lived in the cave all his life and had never committed crimes, so he did not need to repent. He became proud and began to see others as inferior and corrupt beings.

The devil and an evil spirit could not stand his undeserved fame. After all, he was one of them: a thief and murderer. But he was venerated, and they were hated by people.

They began to look for some old habit or inclination in the old man. They found nothing; he had buried his greed, cruelty, and depravity deep. They thought long about how to approach his soul. And they came up with a plot.

The devil, taking the form of a cat, sought refuge in the monk's cave on a tempestuous night, mewling piteously. The hermit, moved by compassion, allowed the creature in.

The cat settled in the cave. It slept during the day, hunted mice at night, and in the evening purred melodies by the fire.

These songs evoked in the monk visions of a peaceful life by a familial hearth, surrounded by children and loved ones. This enraged him; his cruel heart never had room for such human joys. They were abhorrent to him then and now. He grabbed the cat by the tail and threw it out of the cave.

The devil and the evil spirit laughed with satisfaction at making the monk show his true soul.

Then it was the turn of the evil spirit. He transformed into a beautiful young woman. And when the old man cast his nets into the sea to fish, the evil spirit slipped into them. The monk pulled the nets ashore and found a young woman, barely covered with remnants of clothing, lying with her eyes closed, fresh, attractive, and tempting.

Surprised, the old man hurried to help her regain consciousness. The young woman sighed, opened her eyes, and looked tenderly at the monk. He smiled at the young woman and sat beside her. He wanted to ask who she was and how she had ended up in his nets, but the young woman put her hands on his shoulders and kissed him passionately on the lips. The

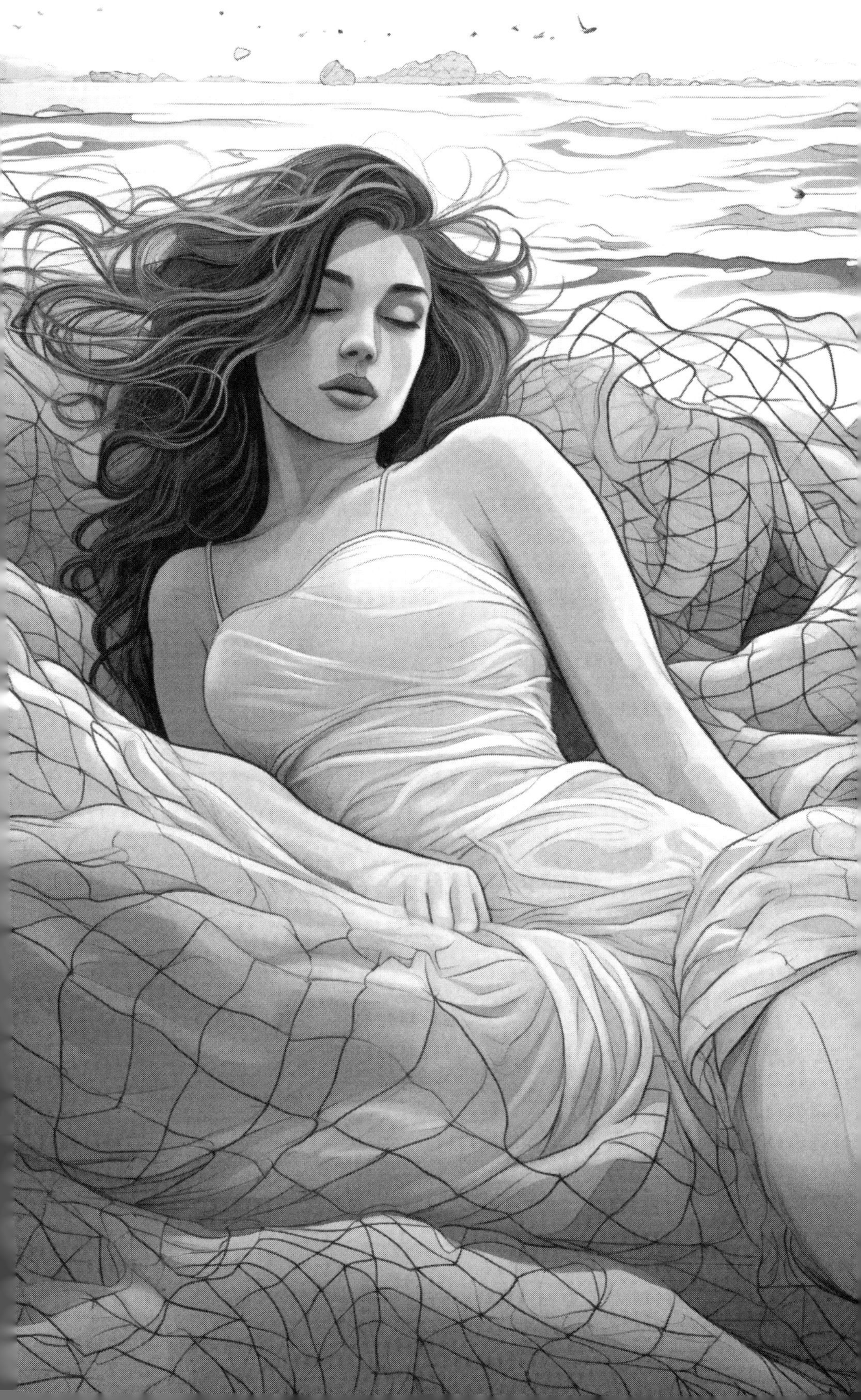

past awoke in the monk, and he pulled her towards him eagerly.

The devil and the evil spirit laughed with satisfaction, forcing the old man to show his true soul once more. Their laughter boomed like thunder.

But the Forces of Good would not tolerate this mockery of the sacred: the family home and pure love. They could no longer tolerate the monk's deceit. And as punishment, they petrified the trio into stone

Thus, near the sea now stand Diva's Rock and Monk's Rock, forever locked in their silent vigil, with Cat Mountain looming behind, an eternal sentinel.

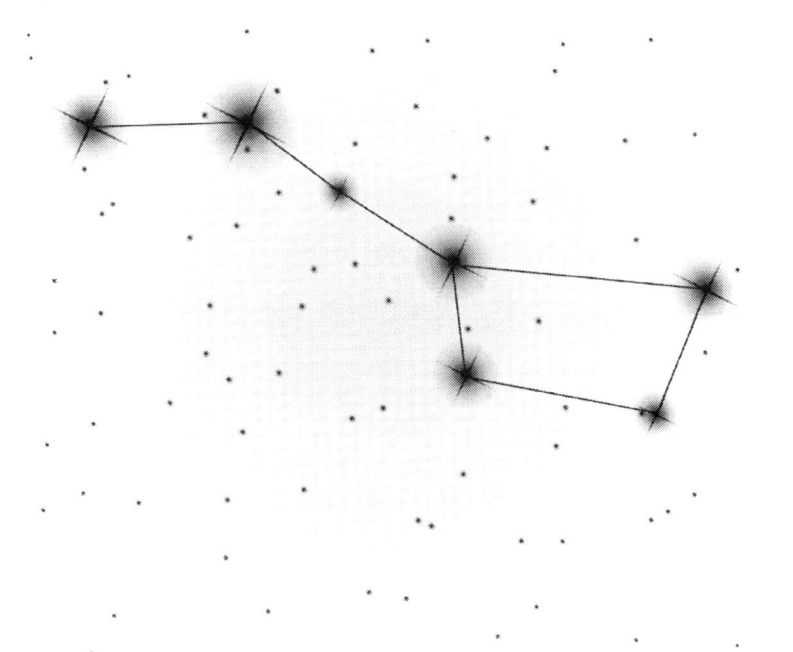

The Legend of the Big Dipper

Long ago, in a place lost to memory, a severe drought ravaged the land. Water vanished from rivers, lakes, and even wells. Without water, people began to fall ill and perish.

In one of these thirsty villages, a widow with her daughter lived. The widow, stricken by thirst, became gravely ill, and her daughter embarked on a quest for water to save her.

After days of searching, the daughter found a small spring. The girl took out a jug and filled it with water. On her journey home, she shared the water with seven thirsty travelers, saving their lives, but only a drop of water remained in the jug.

Exhausted, the girl paused to rest, but a dog, also desperate for water, approached and accidentally knocked over the jug.

Suddenly, seven

bright stars and one smaller one flew out of the jar and soared into the sky. We now know these stars as Big Dipper.

The seven big stars represent the souls of the travelers whom the girl saved, and the little star is the soul of the dog.

Witnessing this act of pure kindness, God chose to honor the girl's generosity. He set these stars in the sky as an eternal testament to her virtue and, as a divine recompense, blessed the thirsty earth with rain.

The Mystery of the Moon

In an era forgotten, the moon shone in the sky with a pure and immaculate light, without spots or marks.

On Earth, two brothers inherited fertile land from their father. Alas, he departed this life without dividing the inheritance between them. Driven by pride and avarice, animosity took root in their hearts, each coveting the larger

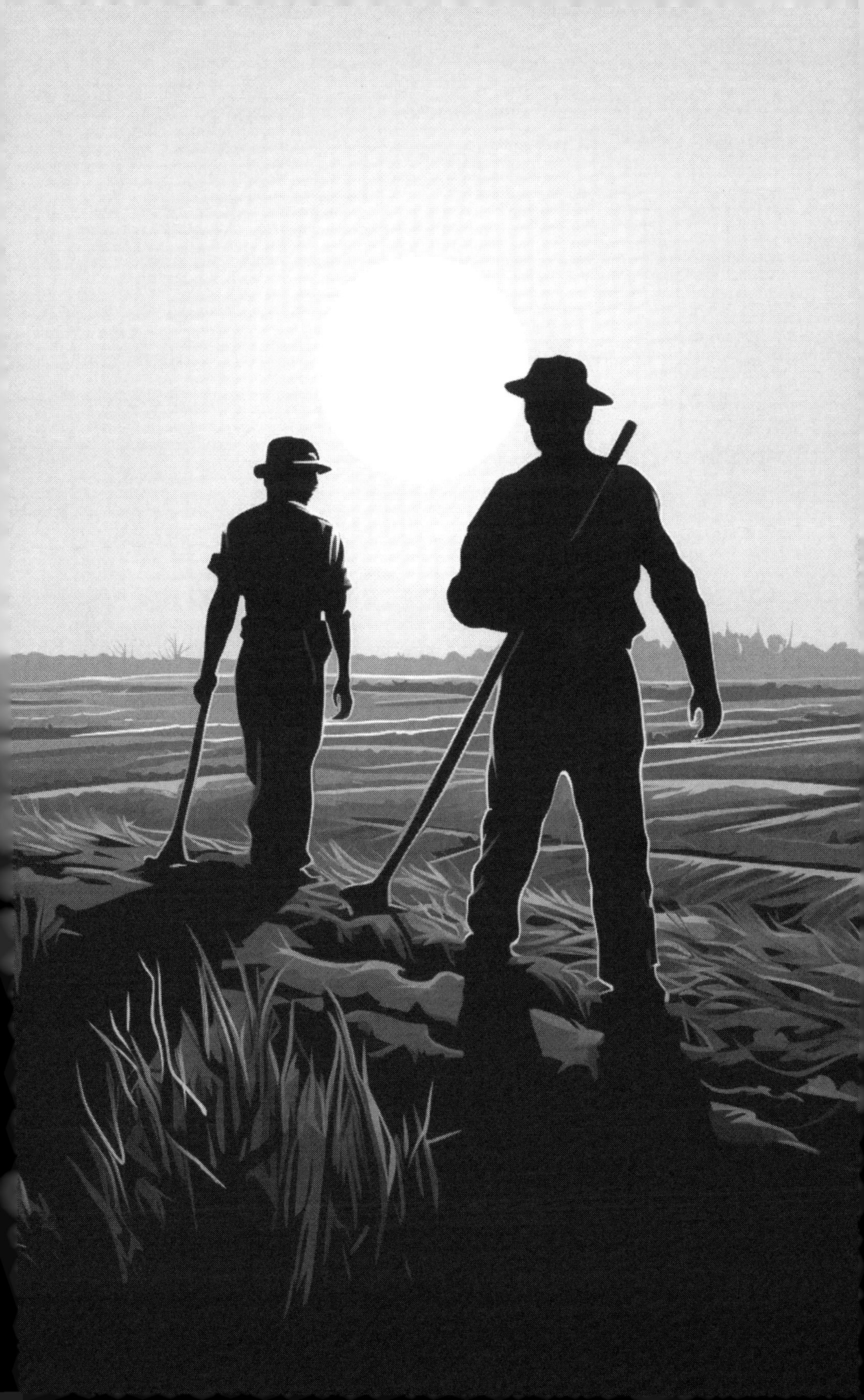

share of their father's legacy.

Under the glow of a moonlit night, as they worked in their fields, the elder brother, consumed by rage, struck down his sibling with a pitchfork. To conceal his vile act, he cast the body into the abyss of a deep well.

When he raised his eyes to the moon, he beheld a stark change: dark blotches marring its once unblemished surface, as though depicting his fratricide.

From that night forth, the elder brother found no peace, despite possessing the entire paternal inheritance. He especially hated moonlit nights, a reminder of his grievous sin.

Even today, with a dash of imagination, one can see on the moon two men armed with pitchforks, facing each other, as in an eternal confrontation.

Why is seawater salty?

Many years ago in a village, there lived two brothers. The younger one was poor, while the elder enjoyed the wealth left behind by their parents. Upon their parents' passing, the elder brother claimed the entire inheritance, leaving the younger in poverty with his wife.

One day, faced with a dire lack of provisions, the younger brother sought assistance from the elder, who heartlessly turned him away.

Disheartened, the younger brother set out to fish, hoping for a fortunate catch. Fortune, however, was not on his side, and he returned without a single fish. On his way back, he stumbled upon some millstones and, with nothing else to show for his efforts, he brought them home.

At home, he recounted his fruitless endeavor to his wife and showed her the stones. In a fit of despair over his inability to provide, he struck the stones, which, to his amazement, began to spin and produce salt. As they spun faster, they generated an ever-increasing bounty of salt. This unexpected fortune allowed the man and his wife to sell the salt and live in comfort.

When the elder brother heard of the

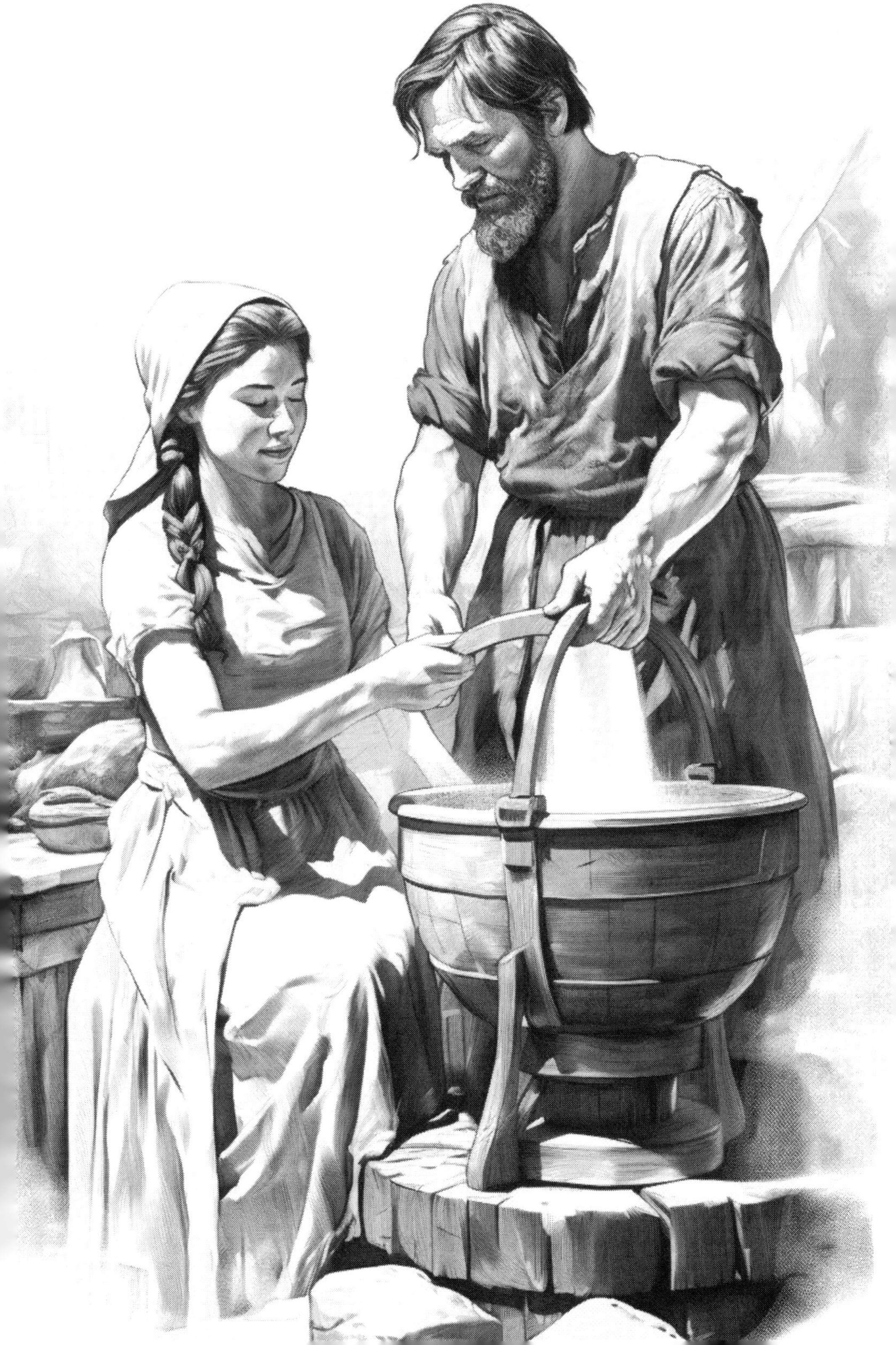

miraculous stones, he demanded to borrow them. The younger brother, albeit with hesitation, consented. But once the elder brother set the stones spinning, he could not stop them. Salt piled up, reaching the ceiling and cracking the walls.

In panic, fearing the destruction of his house, the elder brother rolled the relentless stones down a hill where they plunged into the sea.

To this day, it is said, the stones continue their ceaseless grinding at the bottom of the sea, explaining why its waters are forever salty.

How a mother became a cuckoo

In a distant village, there lived a close-knit family: a fisherman father, a devoted mother, and their children. The family thrived in harmony until tragedy struck and the father succumbed to a grave illness.

With the father gone, the mother toiled ceaselessly to fend for her children. She took to fishing, laboring doubly hard, until she, worn by grief and effort, fell ill.

Lying in bed, unable to move, and with nothing to feed the children, she said to them with a weak voice, "My little ones, give me water. I cannot get up by myself, and I am so thirsty."

"There is no water in the house," the children replied.

"Take the jug to the river and return with water," she coaxed.

The eldest son responded:

"I have no boots; let sister go."

"Go, daughter, and bring me water," she said to the daughter.

"I have no scarf to cover myself. Let the youngest go."

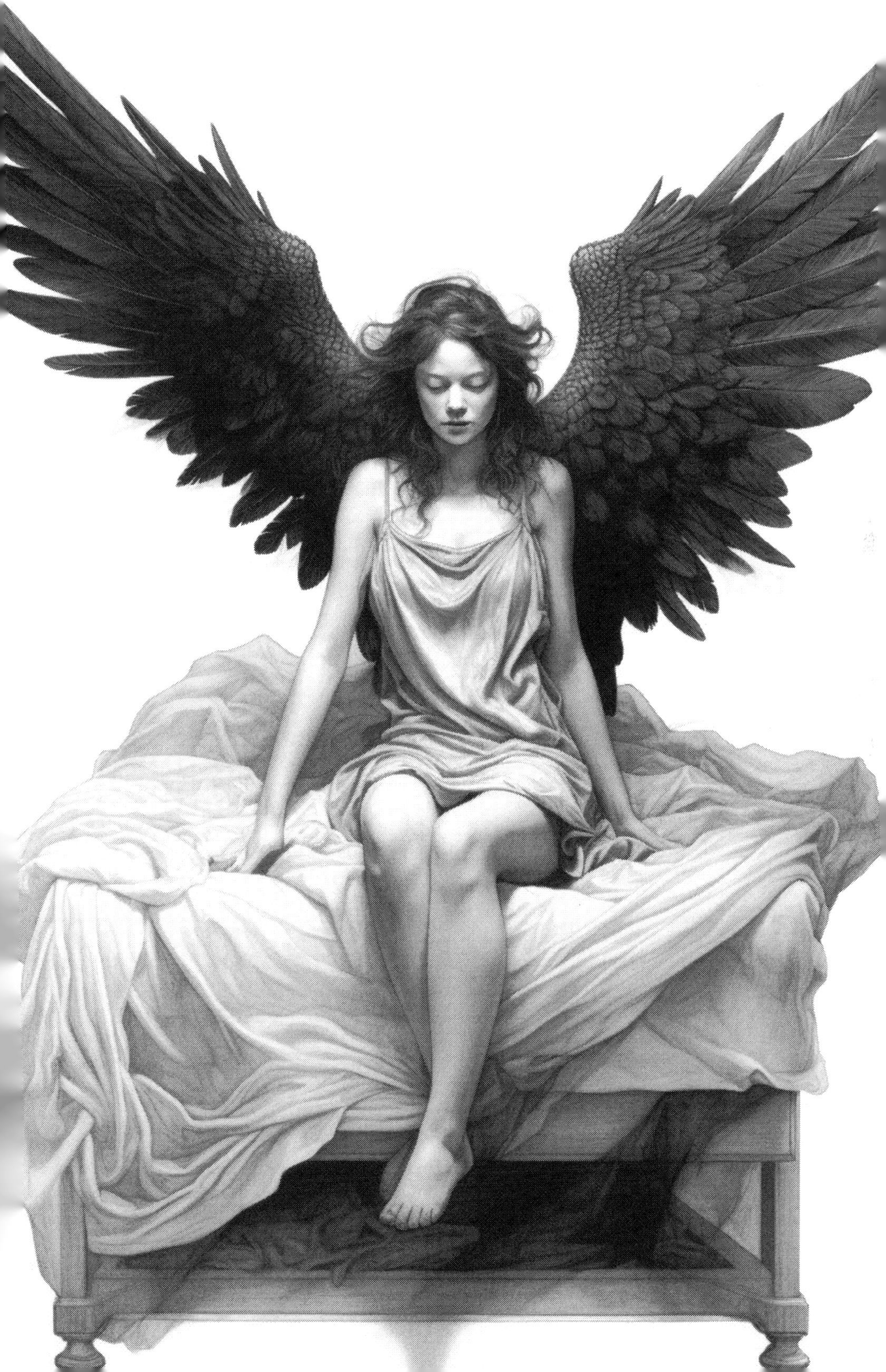

The mother asked the youngest son:

"Son, bring me some water."

"I have nothing to wear," he replied.

So, none of them brought water to the sick mother.

The selfish children went out to play while the mother, with great difficulty, got out of bed as feathers began to grow on her.

The youngest son, returning, beheld the transformation. "Our mother becomes a bird!" he cried, urging his siblings to haste.

He started calling his siblings:

"Look, our mother is turning into a bird!" he exclaimed. "We must save her!"

Seized by urgency, they gathered a jug, a cup, a bucket—anything to carry water. They hastened to the river, shouting in unison,

"Mama, drink!"

But it was too late. The mother, now a cuckoo, could only respond in melancholic calls, "Cu-cu... Too late, children... Cu-cu..."

And she started to fly away. The children ran after her, but the bird was faster. They ran until their bare feet bled.

The mother, eternally a cuckoo, was lost to them, leaving behind only her sorrowful echo.

Today, deep within Ukraine's forests, grows moss with crimson tips—said to be dyed by the blood of the remorseful children's steps.

Where is the True Happiness?

Long ago, there lived a man of wealth, graced with health, a beautiful wife, a strong son, and a daughter of extraordinary beauty. His life was an unceasing celebration of luxury and opulence.

One night, returning from a feast, he met an

old man of simple attire but eyes that sparkled like stars. Intrigued, the wealthy man inquired, "Good evening! Why do your eyes gleam brighter than the stars themselves?"

"It is happiness that kindles them," the old man replied with a smile.

"Happiness?" scoffed the rich man. "How can you claim happiness in such squalor?"

The old man shook his head, "You possess everything but happiness... You have no happiness." With those words, he went on his way, leaving a profound impact.

The wealthy man returned to his palace but found no rest, haunted by the old man's insight. Despite his fortune, happiness eluded him.

After countless restless nights, he embarked on a secretive quest for true happiness.

On his journey, he met an injured man,

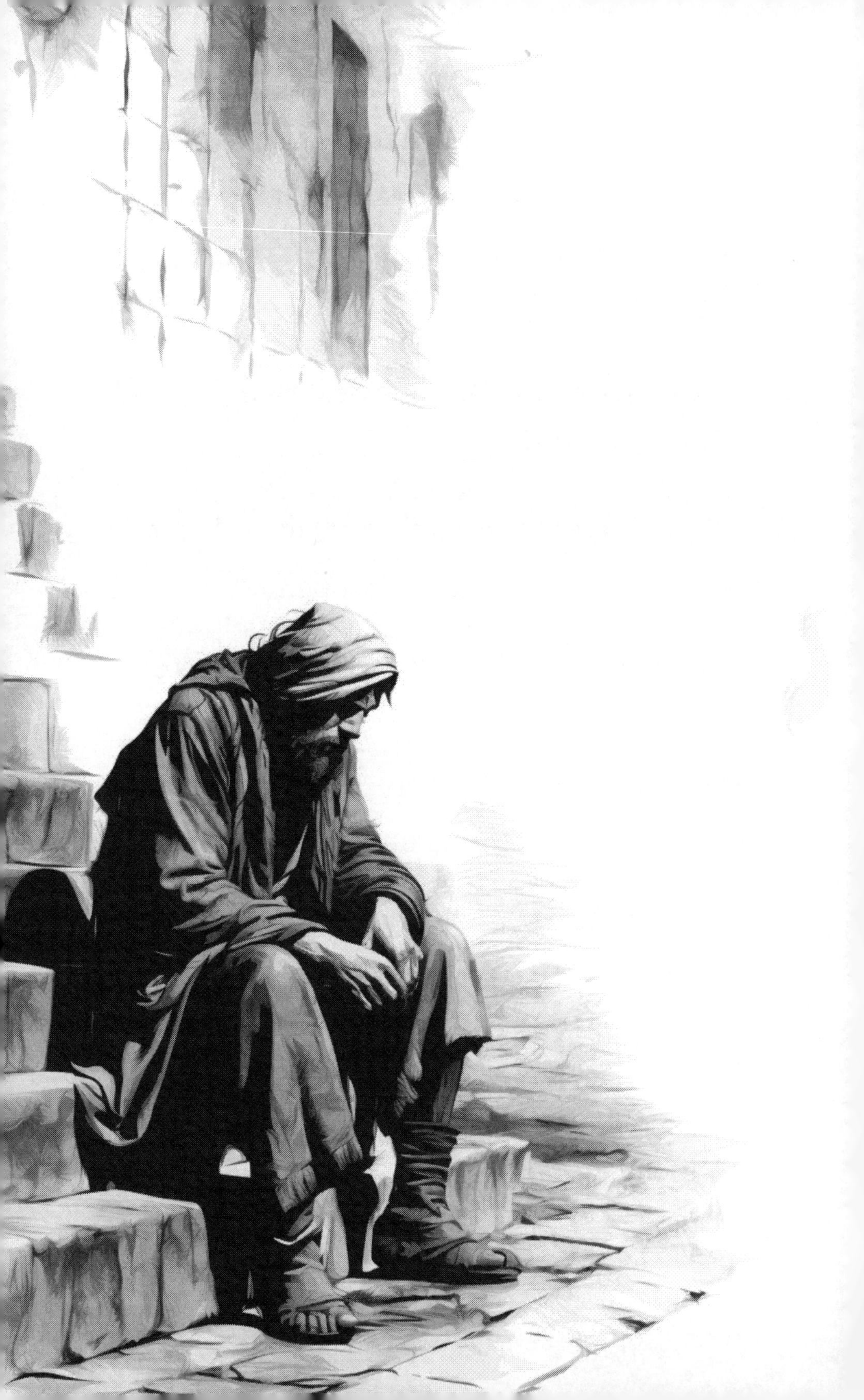

missing a leg, three fingers, and an eye.

"Perhaps he knows," the rich man mused and asked, "Where is happiness found?"

The man replied with a sardonic smile, "Happiness? It's in health, my naive friend!" Disgruntled, he threatened the wealthy man with his cane.

Reflecting, the rich man disagreed, "No, it's not in health; I am healthy but unhappy."

Continuing his search, he encountered a beggar and inquired about happiness after offering a coin.

The beggar asserted, "It's in wealth, without a doubt!"

Yet the rich man knew better, "Money hasn't brought me happiness."

Further along, he found a mourning woman

in black. Her tearful eyes suggested she might know where happiness lies.

When asked, she answered through tears, "Happiness lies in family. I once had it all, but war and sickness have robbed me of mine."

The wealthy man left in silence convinced that even family wasn't the key to happiness.

His journey lasted long, and he had neglected both his family and his businesses. During his absence, his wife had left him and married another, while his children grew up and went far away in search of opportunities.

The man, now alone and sick, arrived at an abandoned hut by the ocean.

On a dark and starless night, he lay down sad and tired. He thought about his past life, the futile search for happiness, and the old man he had met. As he mentally bid farewell to his life, he felt his heart weakening.

"This is the end," he thought.

In the morning, the man woke up with a bright ray of sunlight. As soon as he opened his eyes, he sneezed! And the dust fell from him, the old man...

He looked at the warm and yellow sun and

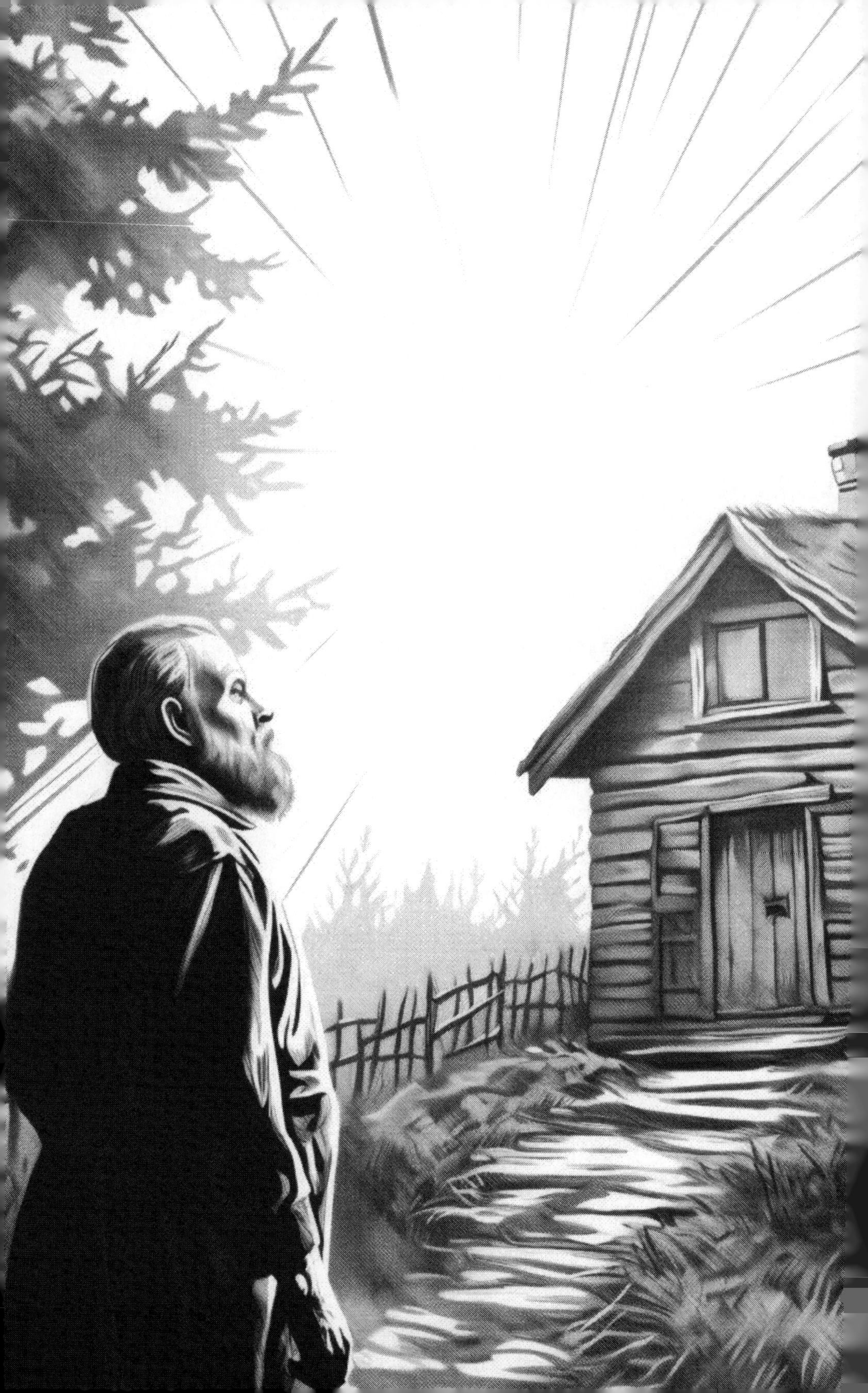

smiled for the first time since he began his journey. For the first time since he saw the old man.

And he felt so light, so calm, so comfortable that even tears of joy sprouted.

And at that moment, he felt happy. For the first time in his life. There it was, happiness.

He sat on a bench, puzzled by this unexpected feeling, and he understood:

NEVER WAIT FOR EVERYTHING TO BE PERFECT! SOMETHING IS ALWAYS MISSING:

MONEY, HEALTH, LOVE... IN THE SEARCH FOR THIS, WE FAIL TO REALIZE WHAT WE HAVE... AND WE DO NOT KNOW HOW TO ENJOY WHAT WE HAVE... IT'S NOT THE ONE WHO HAS EVERYTHING WHO IS HAPPY, BUT THE ONE WHO CELEBRATES WHAT THEY HAVE.

With this epiphany, he viewed the world

anew, his smile as radiant as the old man's eyes, which had once set him on this life-altering path.

The Legend of Destiny

In a small village, two brothers led very different lives. The older one owned vast fields of wheat, while the younger one barely got by with his modest plot of land.

One night, after the harvest, the younger brother went out to check his field. To his surprise, he discovered a young woman picking spikes from his land and taking them to his brother's stacks.

Intrigued, he approached her and asked why she was doing this. The young woman introduced herself as the Fortune of the older brother, who diligently served his interests.

Confused, the younger brother asked about his own Fortune, and the young woman explained that his Fortune was to be found in the market.

He quickly went to the market in search of his Fortune. There, a woman approached him and, after a brief conversation, gave him three coins and advice on how to invest them wisely. She also told him to ask for a horse from his brother.

Motivated by these words, the younger brother followed the advice, took a horse from his brother's stable, and migrated alone to the city. Soon became one of the region's wealthiest

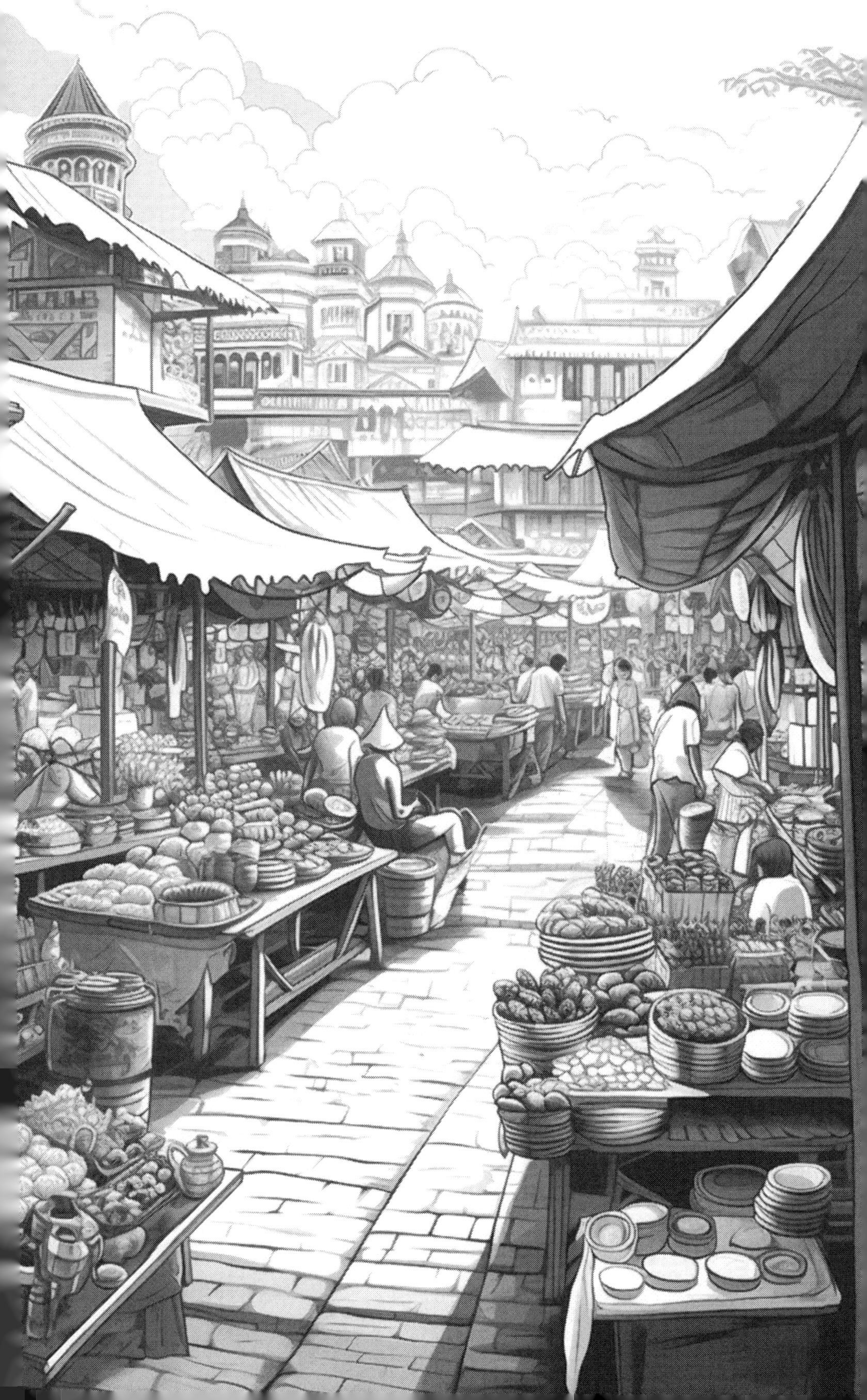

merchants.

Having achieved success, he decided to return to his village with his family. He introduced himself as a wealthy merchant to his brother and requested lodging for a few days, keeping his new identity secret.

They shared news and memories of the village. The older brother talked about his missing brother, complaining that he had taken his horse and left without a trace.

The younger brother inquired about the missing brother's family. The older brother explained that his wife now sold tobacco to support the family.

Moved, the younger brother asked for the woman to be called. When she arrived, she immediately recognized the younger brother as her husband.

Once his identity was revealed, the younger decided to take back his wife and take her with him. He offered his brother to choose a horse from his property as a reward.

The older brother, envious of his brother's transformation, decided to sell everything and move to the city to start a life as a merchant.

Ruined and humiliated, he had to return to the village and ask for his brother's help. The younger brother welcomed him into his home, and the two families lived together happily.

Leaf and gold

Once upon a time, in the lands of Galitzia, the wise King Danylo ruled. He was a great ruler and had immense wealth.

He had a master blacksmith, an exceptional goldsmith, who made the best gold and silver coins in the kingdom.

This craftsman worked in a heavily guarded

chamber under the strict supervision of the king.

Every morning, the king would open the hall for the artisan to enter and work, immediately locking the door behind him.

Danylo was the only one who knew the true value of his treasure, and the artisan, surrounded by the shine of metal, began to believe that only gold had true value.

One day, they began to argue about what was more important: bread or gold. The master craftsman claimed that gold was the true king, but Danylo believed that bread was the foundation of life.

The argument grew louder, and the next day the king saw an inscription on the wall of the workshop: "Bread is mud, the most important things are silver and gold."

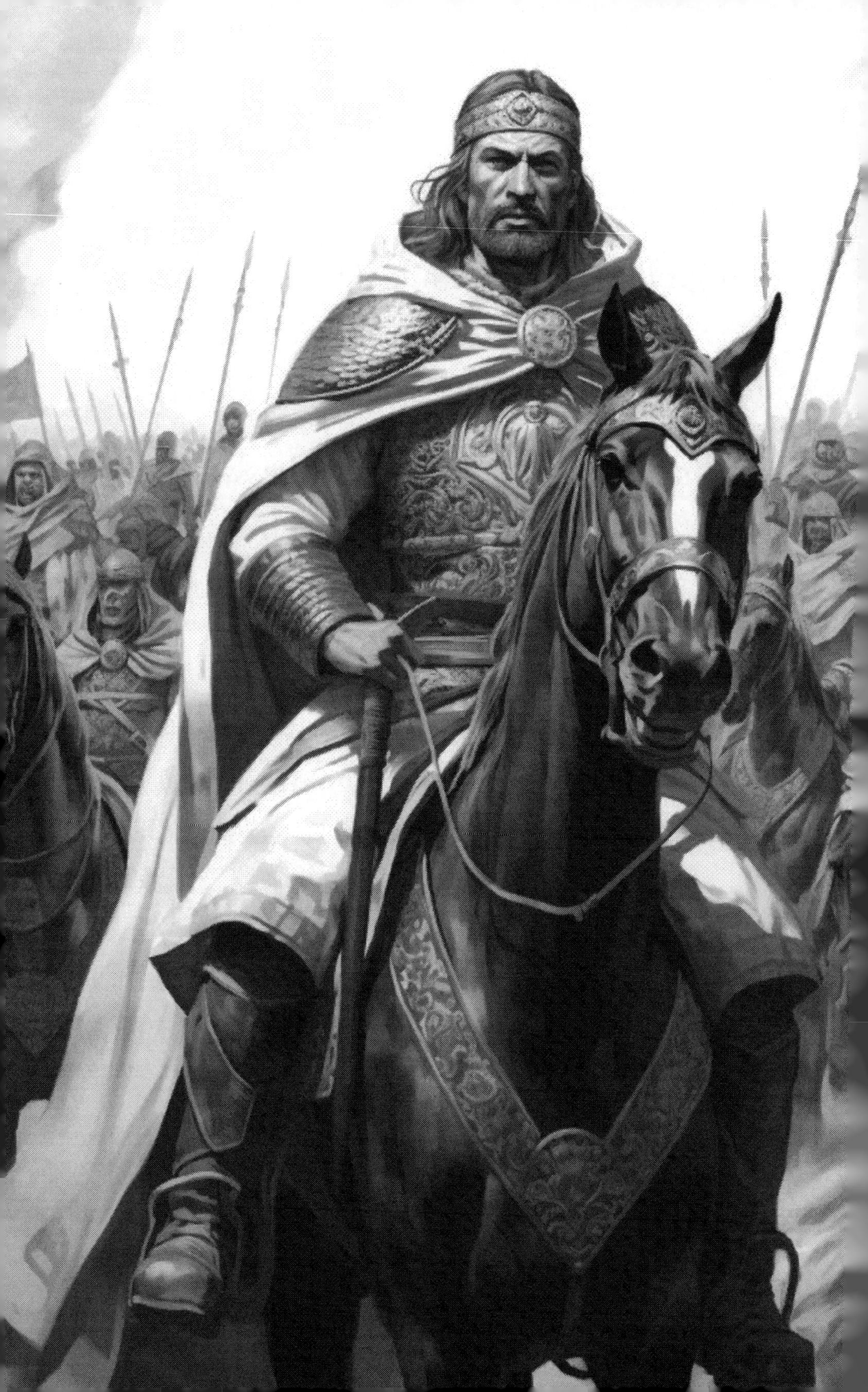

The king saw the inscription but said nothing. The next morning, as usual, he took the artisan to the room where he worked and locked him in.

Suddenly, a messenger brought bad news. A large and threatening enemy was approaching.

It was time to prepare for combat. So, Danylo gathered an army and went to defend his homeland, but he completely forgot about the master craftsman. The king had given strict orders not to open the door of the artisan's workshop. Anyone who disobeyed would be punished with death.

Months passed. Danylo and his army returned home with an epic victory.

However, the craftsman did not appear to celebrate the victory or honor the king. And it was at that precise moment that Danylo remembered. He quickly jumped off his horse

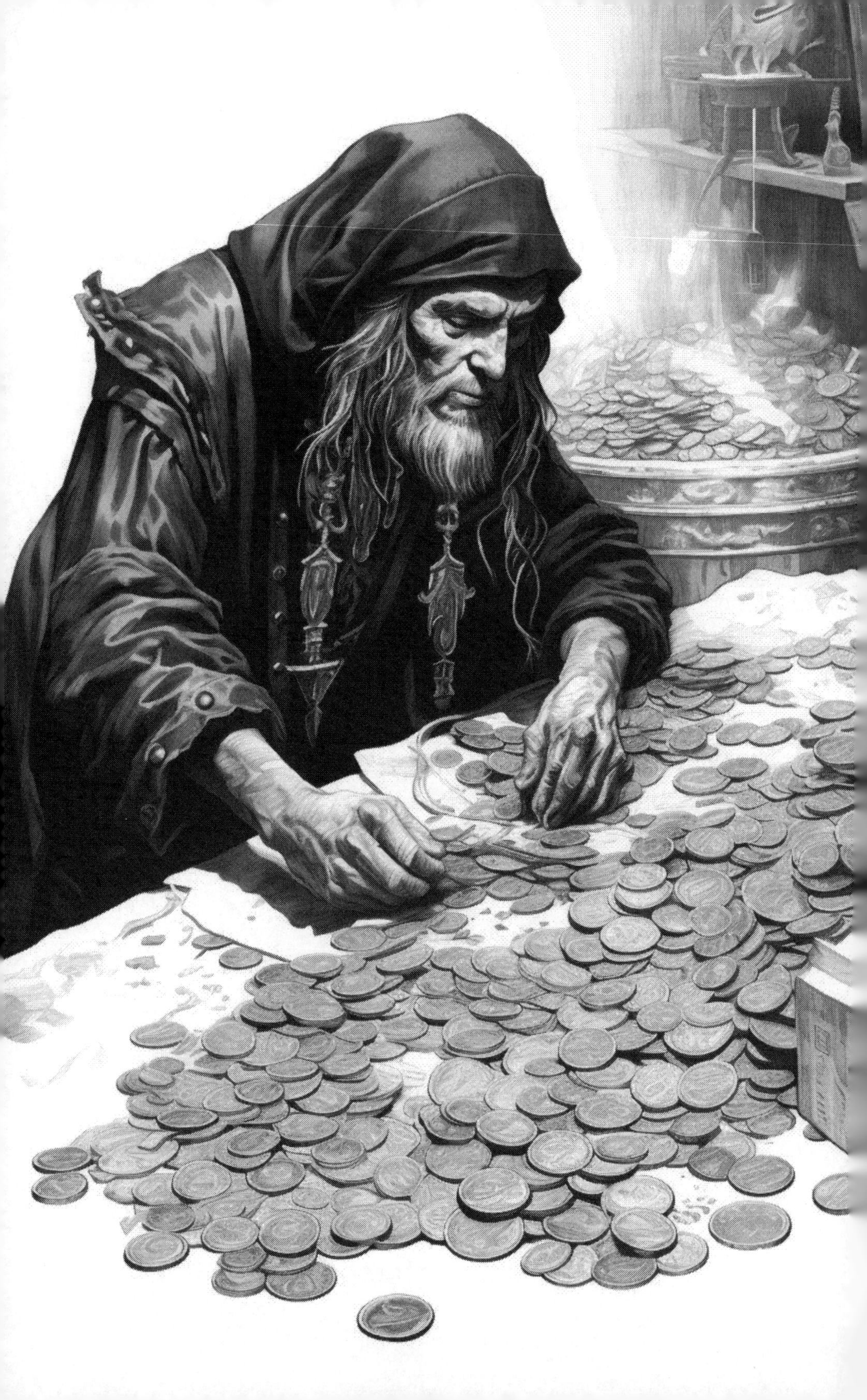

and ran to the room where the master craftsman worked, opened it, and found a skeleton in a pile of gold, all that remained of the master.

And on the wall was written in gold:

"Silver and gold are mud, bread is the king."

Yes, life teaches us to appreciate what matters most.

Founders of Kyiv

In ancient times, when the world was young and secrets were still hidden deep in the forests, in what is now known as Ukraine, sovereigns and sages ruled their clans in harmony with nature.

There were four brothers: one named Kiy, the

second Shchek, the third Khoriv, and the girl Lybed.

Kiy, the eldest and most sagacious, founded his stronghold upon a lofty hill, where Borichev would later rise.

Schek, stubborn and strong, settled on another mountain, which is now known as Shchekovitsa.

Khoriv, brave and resilient, chose the third mountain for himself, which was later named Khorevitsa in his honor.

These siblings, united by strong family bonds and a common goal, built a small village. They called it Kiev, in honor of the eldest brother, as a sign of respect and love. This village, surrounded by vast impenetrable forests, witnessed their wisdom and strength, a place where hunt was noble, and harvests were bountiful.

Ultimately, Kiy returned to his native Kyiv, where he lived out the rest of his days alongside his siblings Shchek, Khoriv, and his sister Lybed.

Their names remained etched forever in the memory of the people, becoming an eternal symbol of courage, wisdom, and harmony with nature, which they so respected.

The End